To the Reader . . .

"World Cities" focuses on cities as a way to learn about the major civilizations of the world. Each civilization has at its roots the life of one or more cities. Learning about life in the great cities is essential to understanding the past and present of the world and its people.

People live in cities for many reasons. For one thing, they value what cities can offer them culturally. Culture thrives in all cities. It is expressed in visual arts, music, and ethnic celebrations. In fact, a city's greatness is often measured by the richness of culture that it offers those who live there.

Many people choose to live in cities for economic reasons. Cities offer a variety of jobs and other economic opportunities. Many city dwellers have found prosperity through trade. Nearly all the world's great cities were founded on trade—the voluntary exchange of goods and services between people. The great cities remain major economic centers.

City living can, of course, have its disadvantages. Despite these disadvantages, cities continue to thrive. By reading about the people, culture, geography, and economy of various metropolitan centers, you will understand why. You will also understand why the world is becoming more and more urban. Finally, you will learn what it is that makes each world city unique.

Mark Schug, Consulting Editor
Co-author of *Teaching Social Studies in the Elementary School* and *Community Study*

CONSULTING EDITOR

Mark C. Schug
Professor of Curriculum and Instruction
University of Wisconsin-Milwaukee

EDITORIAL

Amy Bauman, Project Editor
Barbara J. Behm
Judith Smart, Editor-in-Chief

ART/PRODUCTION

Suzanne Beck, Art Director
Carole Kramer, Designer
Thom Pharmakis, Photo Researcher
Eileen Rickey, Typesetter
Andrew Rupniewski, Production Manager

Reviewed for accuracy by:
Barbara Radner
Director of Center for Economic Education
De Paul University

Quoted material on pages 23 and 57 from *Chicago: Metropolis of the Mid-Continent* by Irving Cutler.
© 1982 by Kendall/Hunt Publishing Co. Used by permission.

Excerpt from "Chicago" from *Chicago Poems* by Carl Sandburg, copyright 1916 by Holt, Rinehart and Winston, Inc. and renewed 1944 by Carl Sandburg, reprinted by permission of Harcourt Brace Jovanovich, Inc.

Quoted material on page 26-27 from *People, Space and Time: An Introduction to Community History for Schools* by Gerald Danzer and Lawrence McBride, ©University Press of America.

Copyright ©1990 Raintree Publishers Limited Partnership

Library of Congress Number: 89-10432

1 2 3 4 5 6 7 8 9   93 92 91 90 89

Library of Congress Cataloging in Publication Data

Davis, Jim, 1940-
  Chicago.
  (World cities)

  Summary: Explores the history, cultural heritage, demographics, geography, and economic and natural resources of Chicago.
  1. Chicago (Ill.)—Juvenile literature. [1. Chicago (Ill.)]
I. Hawke, Sharryl Davis. II. Title. III. Series: Davis, Jim, 1940- . World cities.
F548.33.D38 1989 917.73′11   [B] [92]   89-10432
ISBN 0-8172-3025-4 (lib. bdg.)

**Cover Photo: Third Coast Stock Source /
© Ralf-Finn Hestoft**

WORLD CITIES

CHICAGO

CITIES

JAMES E. DAVIS
AND
SHARRYL DAVIS HAWKE

RAINTREE PUBLISHERS
Milwaukee

Contents

Introduction

Amazing Chicago!

The introduction to this book is called "Amazing Chicago!" for several good reasons. First, the city has a great location. Look at a map of North America. You will see that Chicago is located almost in the middle of the continent in the state of Illinois. You will also see that Chicago is located at the southern tip of Lake Michigan, one of the Great Lakes. The Great Lakes empty into the Atlantic Ocean to the east. The rivers in and around Chicago flow to the west. They connect the city to the Mississippi River, which flows into the Gulf of Mexico. Chicago is at the midpoint of this lakes-rivers waterway.

Chicago is an amazing place in which to live. The city is like a quilt, with each cloth patch representing one of more than two hundred different neighborhoods. If you live in a neighborhood that is south of the Chicago River, you are called a South Sider. If you live in a neighborhood north of the Chicago River, you are a North Sider. If you live in the area west of the fork in the Chicago River, then you are a West Sider.

Chicago's neighborhoods are called ethnic neighborhoods. This is because as immigrants entered Chicago, they tended to settle in areas where others from their homelands lived. Soon, whole neighborhoods showed the

Sears Tower, which is 1,454 feet (443 m) high, is the world's tallest building.

Chicago's neighborhoods are famous for their ethnic restaurants.

influence of one or another ethnic group. Although one group dominates, today several ethnic groups usually live in a neighborhood. For example, the Back of the Yards neighborhood on the South Side is mostly Polish, but Irish and Lithuanian people also live there. Other neighborhoods on the South Side were originally settled by immigrants from Ireland. People from China, Italy, and Lithuania also live there. The West Side neighborhoods were settled largely by Italians, Jews from eastern European countries, Bohemians, and Greeks. The North Side neighborhoods were first home to immigrants from Germany, Poland, and Scandinavia.

Over the years, new ethnic and racial groups arrived in the city. They moved into the old neighborhoods. In fact, students who attend Nicholas Senn High School on the city's North Side call their school "The Little United Nations." The families of students who attend classes there came to Chicago from more than sixty different countries.

The neighborhoods have a mixture of houses and apartment buildings. Houses in the older neighborhoods are small. Newer neighborhoods have larger homes. The apartment buildings vary in size. Some of these buildings are called two-flats. This means that each building has two apartments. Other buildings are called three-flats or six-flats. In the neighborhoods close to the lake, there are modern high-rise buildings. These buildings range from ten to sixty stories tall. Large high-rise buildings can have as many as one thousand apartments. As many as fifteen families may live on the same floor in a high-rise.

Chicago's neighborhoods are like towns or villages anywhere in the United States. They have small grocery stores and large supermarkets. They have stores for clothing, shoes, hardware, and all sorts of other things. Some neighborhoods even have shopping malls. Almost every neighborhood has schools, parks, a public library, and churches.

Chicago's neighborhoods are famous for their ethnic restaurants. Chicagoans love to travel to other parts of the city to sample the food at friendly neighborhood restaurants. They travel south to Ninety-fifth Street for Croatian food. Croatia is a region in Yugoslavia. The Chicagoans go north on Clark Street for Middle Eastern food. Or they may go west on Lawrence Avenue for Korean food.

Half-melted snow lines the streets of this North Side neighborhood in the Lincoln Park area. Most of these houses are two-flats, which are divided into two apartments.

The population of Chicago grew rapidly from its beginning. In 1830, only a handful of people lived in the area. Fifty years later, in 1880, the population had climbed to almost one million people. Fifty years after that, in 1930, Chicago had more than three million people. In 1980, the city and its suburbs had grown to more than seven million people. No other city in the history of the world has ever grown so fast. Chicago is the third largest city in the United States. Only New York and Los Angeles have more people.

As thousands of people poured into Chicago, the shape of the city changed just as quickly. Wetlands around the tip of Lake Michigan were filled in. Neighborhoods sprouted up like wildflowers. Chicago's central business district began with a few cabins near the mouth of the Chicago River. Within just a few years, the district spanned both sides of the river. Hotels, stores, factories, and warehouses crowded in. In 1871, after the Great Chicago Fire destroyed a large part of the city, Chicago recovered and became even greater than before.

Today, Chicago is a city on the go. Every working day, starting about 7 A.M., almost one million people travel the expressways and ride on trains into the central business district. If you stand on a street corner, you can hear a humming sound as the city goes about its work. Then, at five o'clock in the afternoon, the people return to their neighborhoods.

Nothing stays the same in Chicago for long. The business district is constantly changing. Old buildings are torn down; new ones are put up in their places. Old warehouses are re-

Chicago's morning traffic carries almost one million people into the city's central business district each workday.

People crowd the sidewalks along Michigan Avenue, a part of downtown that is near the city's lakefront.

modeled into luxury apartments. Meanwhile, one ethnic group gradually moves out of a neighborhood as a new group moves in.

If you take a trip to Chicago, you will see how its great location, its people, and its constantly changing shape make it an amazing place. The city has skyscrapers, museums, sports stadiums, lakes and rivers, and miles of tree-lined streets. One thing is for sure—you'd better be able to move fast if you hope to see Chicago before it changes.

How Did Chicago Start?

When people first settled in Chicago, the land for miles around the tip of Lake Michigan was a muddy swamp. The wetlands made a nice home for birds and animals, but it is hard to imagine how skyscrapers, factories, and neighborhoods appeared on the shore of Lake Michigan.

The Ice Age

Thousands of years ago, giant sheets of ice called glaciers covered the northern part of the continent. This period was called the Pleistocene Ice Age. It started about 1½ million years ago and lasted until about 10,000 years ago. As they moved, the glaciers plowed through land, pushing loose soil and rocks ahead of them. When the glaci-

ers melted, this debris formed low hills called moraines. The moraines surrounded the region at the tip of Lake Michigan, which had also been shaped by glaciers. The water and ice in the lake extended to the moraines.

When the ice melted, the water flowed through gaps in the moraines toward the Illinois and the Mississippi rivers. Many small rivers and streams were also formed in places gouged out by the glaciers. Meanwhile, the water of Lake Michigan pulled back, leaving a flat plain. Because this land is so flat, it does not drain well. The area beyond the moraines is also flat and wet. The Chicago River, the Calumet River, and a few of the small streams carry off some water, but floods cause serious problems when the winter snow melts and after heavy rainfalls.

Since the Ice Age, the Chicago area has had a continental type of climate. This means that there are four seasons. The summer is hot and dry. Autumn tends to be cool and dry. Winter is cold and wet. Spring tends to be cool and wet. For centuries, this climate was perfect for the tall grass that grew in the fertile soil on the lake plain. Oak and elm forests grew along the rivers and streams and around the moraines. The area became a habitat for all sorts of birds, small furry animals, and larger creatures such as foxes, deer, and bears.

Earliest Inhabitants

Indians were the first people to settle in the area. They arrived about eight hundred years ago. Most of them belonged to the Potawatomi tribe. They hunted and traded with other tribes in the Mississippi River valley such as the Sauk, the Fox, and the Illini. The Potawatomi called the area *Checagou*, which means "evil smelling weed." At the time, the air carried a heavy odor of wild onions and rotting garlic plants.

The first white people passed through Checagou in 1673. These were the French-Canadian explorer Louis Jolliet and the French Jesuit priest Pere Jacques Marquette. They travel-

In 1673, Louis Jolliet led the first expedition into what is now Chicago. The earliest maps of this area were drawn by Jolliet's party.

ed up the Chicago River into Lake Michigan on their way to Canada. The explorers were returning home after looking for a water route connecting the Great Lakes to the Mississippi River. They had hoped to find a connected series of rivers, but they could not find an easy route. These explorers made the first map of the area.

A few years later, another famous French explorer, Sieur de La Salle, and his Italian friend, Henry de Tonti,

Chicago developed where the Chicago River joins Lake Michigan. This was an important stop along the route used by French voyageurs traveling south from the Great Lakes to the Mississippi River.

passed through what became Chicago. They, too, were looking for a nonstop route to the great river. Instead, they had to get out of their birchbark canoe and wade through the marsh. The water in the marshes was often up to their necks and full of blood-sucking leeches. Mosquitoes swarmed around as thick as clouds. They carried their canoe and all their goods on their backs. Carrying boats and supplies in this way is called portaging. Of course, La Salle did not find connected rivers that led to the Mississippi either. Such a route did not exist.

Other French people, called voyageurs, soon followed. Voyageurs were hired to transport people and goods from one point to another. Using the Chicago portage route, they carried on trade between French Canada and Louisiana. The voyageurs' canoes could hold more than ten people and carry nearly 1,000 pounds (454 kilograms) of goods. As they traveled the lakes and rivers, the voyageurs stopped at the site of Chicago to obtain furs from the local Indians. In exchange, they gave the Indians manufactured goods from France.

In 1754, a war broke out in North America between the English and the French. The fighting spread across the continent to what is now Illinois. Many of the Indian tribes joined the French forces and fought against the English. This war is called the French and Indian War.

Soon, English soldiers in bright red coats invaded Illinois. They used the Chicago portage to get to Fort de Chartes in southern Illinois. There they attacked French soldiers. In 1763, the war ended. The French had lost. They were forced to give all of Canada and all of their territory east of the Mississippi River to England. Illinois now became an English territory.

Around 1770, a black trader named Jean Baptiste du Sable moved to Chicago. Du Sable's father was French; his mother was a black slave from Africa. He built a sturdy cabin near the mouth of the Chicago River and lived there for twenty years. Finally, a few other traders joined him, and a tiny trading outpost was born on the shore of Lake Michigan.

Illinois and the Northwest Territory

Between 1776 and 1783, the patriots of the American colonies fought the Revolutionary War to win their independence from England. Once again, there was some fighting in the Illinois territory. Soldiers and Indians who fought this war traveled through Chicago, and a famous battle took place at Kaskaskia in southern Illinois. In this 1778 battle, a colonial army led by Colonel George Rogers Clark captured the English fort at Kaskaskia without firing a shot. Clark's efforts helped win the territory for America.

In 1783, England signed a treaty with the new United States of America. England's Illinois territory became part of the Northwest Territory of the United States. Settlers from the east soon poured into present-day Ohio and Indiana which were also part of the Northwest Territory. They crowded out the Indians who lived there. As forests and hunting grounds disappeared, the different Indian tribes banded together to protect their lands from outsiders. War broke out, and the Indians lead by the Shawnee chief, Tecumseh, were defeated. They were forced to give up their land, including the area around Chicago. This cleared the way for settlers to go west to Chicago.

Fort Dearborn

The American government knew that the Chicago portage was important to trade and needed to be protected against Indian attacks. In 1803, the army built Fort Dearborn across the Chicago River from du Sable's cabin. Settlers thought that the fort would keep them safe. They were wrong.

In 1812, the United States was again at war with England. The English joined with the Indians to try to win back their lost territory. Early in the war, the Potawatomi Indians attacked Fort Dearborn and burned it to the ground. About fifty settlers were killed, and those who survived moved away.

The war ended in 1815. Soldiers returned and Fort Dearborn was rebuilt. Slowly, the settlers began to trickle back. But most people who were moving west from the eastern states still feared the Indians. They settled in southern Illinois, which seemed safer. When Illinois became a state in 1818, southern Illinois had a

population of almost forty thousand. At that time only about one hundred people lived in Chicago.

Black Hawk's War

The Indians made their last stand in Illinois in 1832, led by Black Hawk. The United States Army defeated Black Hawk and his warriors. One Illinoisan who later became president of the United States fought in this

Fort Dearborn (left) was built in 1803 to protect settlers from Indian attacks. Conflict with the Indians ended in 1832 with Black Hawk's War. One veteran of this war was Abraham Lincoln (above), who later became president of the United States.

war. He was Abraham Lincoln, a young man from the Illinois state capital of Springfield.

In 1835, about eight hundred Indians gathered near the lakeshore to receive a small amount of money and some goods. Then they crossed the Chicago River and headed west toward the Mississippi River. Chicago had been their homeland for centuries, but they could not turn back the tide of settlers moving west. After the Indians were gone, the land around Chicago was "up for grabs."

WORLD
CITIES

Growth of Chicago to 1893

In 1833, there were about 150 people in the town of Chicago. People began to pour in from the eastern states and from southern Illinois. The newcomers were attracted to Chicago because land and housing were cheap.

Four years later, in 1837, Chicago had four thousand citizens. They formed a city government, built a school, and established several churches. The city limits expanded from an area two blocks long and two blocks wide to an area of 10 square miles (26 square kilometers). What caused this rapid growth?

The Era of Canals

Chicago received its first big economic boost from the Erie Canal.

Opened in 1825, the Erie Canal connected Lake Ontario to the Hudson River. The Hudson River flowed to New York City and the Atlantic Ocean. New York was the country's largest city.

Because of the canal, Chicago was now connected to important East Coast port cities by way of the Great Lakes. This connection would allow Chicago to trade with any of these East Coast cities. If Chicago was to prosper, however, it would have to develop a port of its own. In the 1830s, hundreds of men went to work improving the Chicago River. They cleared away a sandbar that blocked the mouth of the river to make way for the big sailing ships and steamships that traveled on the

Great Lakes. They also built piers for a harbor.

One more task remained. The need for a canal linking Chicago to the Mississippi River was plain for all to see. In 1842, the Illinois and Michigan Canal Company accepted the challenge. Thousands of Irish immigrants were hired to dig a ditch 96 miles (154 km) long. The canal followed along much of the French voyageurs' old portage route, and it took six years to build. When the Illinois and Michigan Canal opened in 1848, it connected the Port of Chicago to the Illinois River, which flowed into the Mississippi River.

The United States now had a continuous water route between the trading cities of the Gulf of Mexico, the Mississippi River valley, the Great Lakes, and the Atlantic Coast. Chicago

In 1848, the Illinois and Michigan Canal opened a direct waterway between the Great Lakes and the Mississippi River.

was located right at the heart of the system. The area near the site of old Fort Dearborn and along the banks of the Chicago River was soon lined with freight warehouses. Sailing ships with tall masts competed with long, flat barges for space on the narrow strip of river water. By the 1880s, more than 26,000 ships docked in the Port of Chicago every year. As trade increased, Chicago prospered.

The Era of Railroads

A few years after the Illinois and Michigan Canal opened, the first train arrived in Chicago. It carried wheat from farms about 10 miles (16 km) to the west. Because there was no place

Railroads provided the link between Chicago, the markets of the East, and the vast farmlands of America's West. By rail, grain was shipped into the city, while finished goods and farm machinery could be shipped west and sold to farm families.

for the train to turn around, the engineer put the train in reverse and backed home!

Chicago's first mayor, William Ogden, was one of the country's first railroad owners. He had many friends who worked in the state and national governments. Together they convinced other owners of early railroads to make Chicago their headquarters. Chicago was soon connected by railroad to the East Coast. Within a few more years, the city was connected to the West Coast by Ogden's own railroad, the Union Pacific.

Railroad lines spun out from the city like the silk pattern of a spider's web. By the end of the century, more than twenty-five major railroad lines ran through Chicago. Dozens of smaller railroad lines crisscrossed the city. Chicago became the railroad capital of the nation.

The railroads provided work for thousands of new Chicagoans. Unskilled laborers did the backbreaking job of constructing the track bed, laying the wooden ties, and hammering the steel rails in place. Freight yards, warehouses, and passenger stations had to be built. Each company needed workers in its downtown office. Other people found jobs working in the factories that manufactured equipment for the railroads. Hundreds of different products were needed. For example, foundry workers in mills made giant steam locomotives. Workers in small shops hand made the lace curtains for the fancy passenger cars.

Many of the unskilled workers who worked on the railroads and the canal were able to save their wages. When they could afford it, they moved west. They bought homesteads and started farms. After they were in their new homes, Chicago still played a big part in their lives, and they remained important to Chicago.

The Era of Industry and Trade

As Chicago grew, so did the farming region of the prairies and the Great Plains. The people who worked in Chicago's factories and businesses depended on the farmers for food.

Farmers, however, had needs the city could meet. For example, they needed equipment to break up the grassy soil on the fertile prairie, plant seeds, and harvest crops. In 1847, Cyrus McCormick built a factory in Chicago to manufacture farm machinery. His planters, mowers, and reapers were not very heavy and not too expensive. His machines helped farmers increase the amount of grain they could produce.

Farmers and cattle ranchers in the West used the new railroads to ship their grain and livestock to Chicago. The food-processing industry became important to Chicago, and mills and grain elevators were built to grind and store grain.

Chicago's most famous food-processing location was the Union Stock Yards. They were built in 1865 when the owners of nine railroads joined forces with the owners of seven important meat-packing companies. Within two years, the stockyards were the largest and busiest in the world.

The Union Stock Yards seemed like a little city. There was a newspaper, a private railroad to bring workers to and from work, a private canal, and a bank. There were offices, hotels, and theaters. Almost thirty thousand people worked in the stockyards. For most of them the work was dangerous, dirty, and smelly.

Chicago's railroads and meat-packing companies together built the Union Stock Yards. This 345-acre (140 ha) sprawl of stockpens and slaughterhouses was on the city's south side.

Chicago Historical Society

Celebration: The World's Columbian Exposition

At the 1893 World's Columbian Exposition, visitors could ride the world's first electric train or listen by telephone to a concert being played in New York City.

In 1893, Chicago played host to people from around the world at a world's fair. The event was held in honor of Christopher Columbus's voyage to the New World some four hundred years earlier. Famous architects and artists planned a tremendous fairgrounds on the South Side. They created snow-white buildings that looked like those of ancient Greece and Rome. They dug lagoons and planted lovely flower gardens in the parks.

The latest scientific inventions were displayed at the fair. Nations from around the globe set up exhibits and sent people dressed in native costumes. There was plenty of entertainment, too. Fair-goers rode on a giant ferris wheel that carried two thousand people at a time. If that was not enough, across the street from the World's Fair, Buffalo Bill's Wild West Show featured cowboys and Indians.

The Columbian Exposition lasted six months. During that time, more than 27 million visitors attended the event. That number was about half the total population of the United States at that time! It was a triumphant end to a half century of rapid change. In 1834, Chicago was only a muddy trading post. Less than sixty years later, it had become one of the greatest cities in the world.

WORLD
CITIES

Life in Chicago

By 1900, all the world knew that Chicago was a great city, the second largest city in the United States. Chicago had hundreds of thousands of people, transportation systems, industry, and trade. The lakefront was beautiful.

But what was life like for children who grew up in this city? What was it like in their neighborhoods? What kinds of jobs did people hold? Where did families go to have fun? Was Chicago a great place for them?

Immigrants Come to Chicago

An immigrant is a person who moves from one country to live in another. During the 1800s, millions of immigrants came from countries in Europe to live in the United States. They crossed the Atlantic Ocean in crowded ships bound for New York City and other ports. From those ports, they spread out across the country.

The Irish and the Germans were the first immigrants to come to Chicago in large numbers. They arrived on boats and on trains. The Irish tended to settle on the South Side of the Chicago River, while Germans often settled on the North Side. People who lived in the city before immigrants arrived did not like them very much. As a result, immigrants stayed close together in their neighborhoods.

Other immigrants from Europe soon followed. People from Poland, Russia,

Italy, Greece, and dozens of other countries poured into the city. More Irish and Germans came, too. Each group moved into its own neighborhood.

Immigration helped increase the city's population. In the 1870s, after the Great Chicago Fire, more than 1,000 immigrants arrived in the city every day. In 1870, the city's population grew to 600,000. By 1900, Chicago had more than 1½ million people.

Chicago burst at the seams. The city had to expand its borders to make space for all the people, so it began to annex nearby towns. This means that the towns officially became part of the city. The great annexations occurred in 1886 and 1889. The city doubled its land area both times.

Life in an Ethnic Neighborhood

Chicago's Near West Side became neighborhoods for many immigrants who made their first Chicago homes there. Trains carrying immigrants stopped at nearby Dearborn Station, where the newcomers spilled out and onto the street. They carried all their possessions in cloth bags. The city area they entered was a strange place. The dirt streets were crowded with people, goats, and horses. There were no trees or other plants anywhere in sight. Wooden houses, stores, and factories were crowded together side by side. By 1900, the houses were in bad condition. Waves of earlier immigrants had worn them out.

The newcomers could not speak English. They needed help from the earlier immigrants to find a place to live. To them, the only familiar sights on the Near West Side were church steeples and synagogues.

Halsted Street divided the Near West Side in half. A woman named Hilda Satt Polacheck who emigrated from Poland remembered what life was like on this street when she was a young girl. Here is what she had to say:

The home to which father brought the family was a six-room flat, the upstairs of a two-story wooden house. The first floor was a steam-ship ticket agency. It was typical of the houses that had been built after the Chicago Fire, just twenty-one years before we arrived. Compared with some of the homes of children that I played with, our home was luxurious. We had a toilet with running water in a narrow hall just outside of the kitchen. One of my playmates, a little girl with two sisters, five brothers, a father and mother, lived in back of a basement grocery story in three rooms.

As Chicago's factories used more and more foreign-born labor, employers began to offer "Americanization" classes for these new immigrants.

The only play space was the sidewalk in front of the house. The sidewalks were wooden planks, which became slimy and slippery after rain. The streets were paved with wooden blocks, after a heavy rainfall, the blocks would become loose and float about in the street.

School and Work in an Ethnic Neighborhood

Schools in the neighborhoods were three-story brick buildings. Coal-burning furnaces kept the students and teachers warm in the winter. Students jumped rope or played baseball in the schoolyards.

Around 1900, students were required to attend school only about one hundred days per year. The school day ended at noon. Most of the students did not complete eighth grade, and only a handful of those who did graduate went on to high school. This was because immigrant familes needed the children to earn wages, and parents did not think that knowledge gained in school would help the family survive.

Children held jobs in factories where they worked after school and into the night. Many factory owners hired children to work on machines that had tiny parts that only children could reach. Some factory owners employed children because they did not have to pay them as much as adult workers.

Many immigrants who came to the Near West Side with skills found jobs right away. Immigrants who had been farmers in the old country and those from cities who did not have special skills found jobs as laborers. They dug canals, worked in the Union Stock Yards, or built railroads.

Women also worked. Some worked as maids and servants in the homes of wealthy people. Others worked as seamstresses at home or in small factories. They sewed buttons on clothes and stitched garments together from pieces of cloth. This was called piece-work

Sweatshop workers were paid according to how many garments they sewed in a day.

because wages depended on how many pieces a worker could complete in a day. The small factories were called sweatshops because they were so cramped and hot in the summertime.

In general, factory work was dangerous. Workers were often injured on the job. They did not have health insurance, as many workers have today. Factory workers in the 1800s and early 1900s had to pay their own medical bills. They received low wages, and they had to work long hours—sometimes up to fourteen hours a day—even on Saturdays. Workers who lost their jobs had a difficult time finding another one.

Fighting for Rights

Workers on the Near West Side and elsewhere organized labor unions. Union workers demanded higher wages, safe working conditions, and an eight-hour workday. When factory owners did not give in, the workers would go on strike. Most strikes in those early days, however, were unsuccessful.

Women also joined unions and went on strike to end the bad conditions in sweatshops. In addition, women known as suffragettes formed organizations to work for the right to vote. In 1913, women in Illinois won the right to vote in presidential elections. It wasn't until 1920 that they could vote in other types of elections.

Groups of suffragettes fought for the right for women to vote. In 1920, the Nineteenth Amendment to the Constitution guaranteed this right.

The city's new immigrants settled into neighborhoods with others who shared their nationality. This Italian travel agency helped Chicago's Italians make arrangements for their relatives to join them in America.

Neighborhood versus Neighborhood

Ethnic groups within the different neighborhoods often kept to themselves. They had their own schools, churches, and meeting places. People felt safest only in their own neighborhoods. Children were afraid to go too far away from home. They knew that gangs in other neighborhoods might try to hurt them if they crossed over the boundary.

Chicago was not a melting pot where all sorts of people eventually blended together. Instead, it was a city with different groups living side by side. Because the groups did not mix together, they did not get to know one another well. Too often, people are afraid of things they do not understand.

Overall, life was not easy for immigrants. The neighborhoods were crowded and unhealthy. Summers were scorching hot, and winters were freezing cold. Few houses had running water or plumbing. Still, many people have fond memories of life in the old neighborhood. After all, this was where they got a fresh start in the New World.

Growth of the Metropolis, 1893-1990

In the years after the World's Columbian Exposition, Chicago continued to grow. New ethnic and racial groups arrived. More industries came to the city. Chicago became a seaport city with the opening of the St. Lawrence Seaway in 1959. With this waterway link, ocean-going ships—not just shipped goods—could reach the city. Through all these changes, Chicagoans tried to find ways to cope.

An Era of Health Reform

Chicago's major health problem involved sewage disposal and clean water. For years, most of the houses in the city did not have toilets. People used privies, or outhouses, behind the houses.

When the city built its first sewage system in the 1880s, waste from homes and businesses was emptied into the Chicago River. The river carried the waste into Lake Michigan. However, the lake was Chicago's source of drinking water. When people drank polluted water, they died of diseases called typhus and cholera.

The city developed a bold plan, creating the Chicago Sanitary District. In 1895, engineers went to work building a new system of drainage canals and waterways. The system was 120 miles (193 km) long. The engineers built locks on the Chicago River that actually made it flow backward. The river now carried sewage and fresh water from Lake Michigan through the new system to the Illinois River. The city hoped that the lake water would dilute the sewage as it carried it away.

An Era of Social Reform

Immigrants continued to pour into Chicago until World War I started in 1914. The new immigrants included people from Austria, Hungary, Russia, the Netherlands, and Slovenia. Like earlier immigrants, the newcomers faced difficult living conditions. Both jobs and housing were hard to find. Housing, when available, often consisted of quick, inexpensive buildings. Quality of life for people in the neighborhoods had to be improved.

One person who tried to help was Jane Addams, a social worker. Addams helped thousands of immigrants learn about life in their new land. She also helped immigrants preserve the ethnic customs of their native lands. As part of this plan, Addams and Ellen Gates Starr opened Hull House—a settlement house—in Chicago. Hull House had workshops, a theater, a library, a large dining room, and meeting rooms. By 1900, almost nine thousand people per day enjoyed activities at Hull House.

Jane Addams and her friends also worked with the city's politicians to make changes in the laws to help all Chicagoans. She wanted new housing, clean city streets, and safe factories. Jane Addams was also worried about children. She wanted schools to stay open in the afternoon, and she wanted students to attend school from September to June. Through her work, Addams saw many of her ideas put into practice.

Ida B. Wells was another important reformer. She was a black woman who settled in Chicago in 1893, the year of the World's Columbian Exposition. At that time, only about one out of every one hundred people in the city was black. Most of them lived on the South Side in crowded, old neighborhoods. The other black families were scattered around the city.

Jane Addams organized Hull House to aid Chicago's immigrants (below).

Carlye Calvin

When more black families began to move to the city around 1914, the other neighborhoods did not welcome them. The blacks were forced to live in a segregated, or separate, neighborhood called the Black Belt. Ida B. Wells was the first black woman lawyer in Illinois. She fought in the courts against segregation. She also fought against racial prejudice in her column in the *Chicago Defender* newspaper.

Migration to Chicago

In 1917 and again in 1941, the United States went to war. Chicago's factories needed workers to produce materials to help win the war. Black people from southern states moved to the northern industrial states to get jobs.

The movement of blacks between the wars is called the Black Migration. At the beginning of World War I, Chicago had about 50,000 black residents. At the end of World War II, the city had more than 400,000. Since then, the black population has climbed to more than one million people out of a total population of 3 million.

The *Chicago Defender* and the Chicago Urban League helped the newcomers find housing and work. But when black families tried to move to better houses outside the Black Belt, hostile whites bombed their new black neighbors' homes. The city remained segregated and tense. In 1919, a race

Click/ Chicago Ltd.—©Brian Seed

riot broke out at a beach on Lake Michigan and spread across the city. The riot lasted a week. In Chicago, forty people were killed and five hundred people were injured so badly that they had to go to hospitals.

Segregation is now forbidden by law in schools, businesses, and all public

Spanish-Speaking Immigrants

The first Spanish-speaking people in Chicago came from Mexico. They left their native country during a political revolution in 1910. They settled near a neighborhood called The Bush. It was located by the steel mills on the South Side.

Since then, there has been a steady flow of Mexicans into the city. Recent

Blacks who migrated to Chicago during the two world wars settled on the city's South Side (left). In an Hispanic neighborhood, a craftsman fashions traditional masks (below).

Click / Chicago Ltd.—©Loren Santow

places. Still, many Chicago neighborhoods have remained racially segregated. As whites moved out of old neighborhoods, blacks moved in. Only a few of the neighborhoods along the lake shore are integrated, or racially mixed.

Mexican immigrants settled in an old Czech neighborhood called Pilsen. Pilsen and other Mexican-American neighborhoods are lively places with colorful murals, or paintings, on the sides of buildings and walls.

Other Spanish-speaking people arrived in Chicago in large numbers after 1960. Puerto Ricans, Cubans, people from Central American countries, and those from the Philippine Islands are the latest newcomers to the city. These groups have settled in North Side neighborhoods. The Puerto Ricans are the largest group, living in the old German neighborhood of Humboldt Park.

These immigrants faced the same sort of problems as the earlier ethnic groups. They moved into old, run-down areas. They had to work at jobs that no one else would take. Wages were low. The city government ignored them. Many of them did not speak English.

In addition, the new immigrant groups did not mix much with each other. Some of their neighborhoods are close together, but each one has its own personality. Many Mexicans who have been in the city for many years now have good jobs. Many Cubans came to the city with good educations. They have also done well.

Since the 1960s, the Spanish-speaking segment of the population has grown rapidly. It has doubled each decade. Today, there are more people in this group than in any other ethnic or minority group in Chicago except for blacks.

Crisis and Confidence

Chicago changed rapidly in the twentieth century. As soon as the city

Image Bank / ©Santi Visalli

solved one problem, other problems cropped up. But Chicago's spirit never dropped.

When the Great Depression hit the country in 1930, Chicago knew just what to do. In 1933, on its one hundredth birthday, Chicago held another world's fair, called the Century of Progress. Once again, millions of people visited the city. Chicagoans showed their guests that they were the most confident people in the world. No problem was too big for Chicagoans to solve.

Murals in the Pilsen area celebrate the Mexican heritage shared by many of this neighborhood's residents.

An Era of Violence

One problem that was not easily solved was violent crime. During the 1920s, a period known as the Roaring Twenties, gangs terrorized some neighborhoods. Italian, German, Irish, and Jewish gangs fought with each other to control illegal gambling and alcohol. Police and judges fought against the gangs, but they did not have much success.

Chicago became known as the most violent city in the United States. Rival

King of the Chicago gangsters was Al Capone (center). Capone is shown here at his trial for the tax evasion charges that would send him to prison.

gangs killed their enemies on the city streets. They bribed crooked city officials to get what they wanted. Gangs also set up regular businesses, and frightened honest Chicagoans into dealing only with them.

Today there are new gangs in the city. Some of them have more than five thousand young people as members. Like the old gangs, they have their headquarters in the neighborhoods. The members are violent. They frighten people into obeying them. Some young people join gangs because they are afraid of what will happen to them if they don't.

The city has found ways to help young people use their time in better ways. The Chicago Park District has parks and fieldhouses in every neighborhood. Children can swim, play games, learn how to play musical instruments, and take trips around the city. The police and fire departments also sponsor activities for children in the neighborhoods.

Politics in Chicago

For many years, Chicago's city government was controlled by a group of politicians known as the "Machine." The Machine helped people who kept these politicians in power. This way of getting things done was called the patronage system. It worked like this. If a person wanted to work in the fire department, or in any other official position, he or she would need a recommendation from a member of the Machine. The city's thirty thousand employees were called the Patronage Army. The were loyal to the Machine.

If an immigrant needed a job, a member of the Machine would help him find one. In return, the immi-

Mayor Richard J. Daley ran the city of Chicago from 1955 until his death in 1976.

grant was expected to vote for the Machine's political candidate in the next city's election. If a businessman needed a street paved for his factory, he would contribute money to the Machine's election campaign treasury. These ways of doing things are illegal.

Chicago has a representative form of government. The city has fifty wards. Each ward elects one alderman to the city council. The mayor of the city represents all of the people. When the Machine was powerful, forty-nine out of fifty aldermen were part of it.

From 1955 until 1976, Chicago's mayor was Richard J. Daley. The people loved Mayor Daley, voting him into office in four elections in a row. While Daley was mayor, Chicago was known as "The City That Works."

In 1983, Harold Washington became Chicago's first black mayor. Here, Washington (right) is sworn into office. Former Mayor Jane Byrne (to Washington's left) also attended the ceremony.

Mayor Daley saw what was great about Chicago and made those things even greater. During his terms, the city built the world's busiest airport, O'Hare International. A new Port of Chicago was constructed on the south shore of Lake Michigan. The central business district was filled with towering skyscrapers. City workers made Chicago one of the cleanest and most beautiful cities in the world.

In 1979, Jane Byrne became the first woman mayor of Chicago. Another first for the city occurred in 1983. In that year, Harold Washington was elected mayor. He was the first black mayor in Chicago's history. Mayor Washington wanted to make life better in the neighborhoods. He worked hard to help blacks and whites understand each other. He broke up the old Machine. He thought that the city government should work for all the people, not just for people on the inside.

Mayor Washington died in 1987. Eugene Sawyer, who is also black, then became mayor. Then in 1989, Richard M. Daley defeated Sawyer in the race for mayor. Richard M. Daley is the son of the late Richard J. Daley.

WORLD CITIES

Growth of the Suburbs

Communities around a large city are called suburbs. The city and the suburbs together are called the metropolitan area. From the beginning, small towns grew up around Chicago. Most of them, however, developed after 1920, when Chicago began to run out of space for more building.

Some of the suburbs around Chicago are just about as old as the city itself. A few, like Joliet, are older. As Chicago expanded in the late 1800s, the city annexed several of the early suburbs. These suburbs, such as Hyde Park on the South Side and Lake View on the North Side, became important city neighborhoods. Since the 1930s, however, people in suburbs next to the city have not wanted to be annexed.

Roads, Railroads, and the Suburbs

Roads connected the early suburbs to the city. Some of the roads followed Potawatomi Indian trails. Little Fort Road, now Lincoln Avenue, eventually led north to Waukegan. Vincennes Avenue was built along a trail that ended at the Ohio River, far to the southeast. Chicago Road went northeast to Detroit. The towns along these roads were farming communities.

When the railroads came to Chicago, towns developed every few miles along the tracks. People lived in these towns, but they kept their jobs in the city. Every workday, they walked to the train station and rode the train to and from Chicago. The railroads made

through the town center. Living in Riverside is like living in a park.

Some industries followed the railroads to the suburbs. The Western Electric Company, which manufactured electrical equipment and telephones, built a large factory in Cicero. The Libby, McNeill & Libby foodprocessing company built a plant in Blue Island. The Pullman Company, which made railroad cars, was in a town named Pullman. Oil refineries

Many Polish and Bohemian residents live in suburban Berwyn (left). Frederick Law Olmsted designed Riverside, which is a parklike suburb of the city.

it easier for farmers near these towns to get their produce to city markets. By 1900, towns were strung out on the railroad routes like charms on a bracelet.

Most of these towns were residential suburbs. The houses were large, and there was plenty of room for children to play. One of the suburbs is Riverside. It was planned by a landscape architect named Frederick Law Olmsted in 1869. He designed a town with curved streets, large lots, and open spaces. Not far from the railroad station, the Des Plaines River flows

Just north of the city is the lakefront suburb of Evanston, famous as the home of Northwestern University.

were built near Joliet and in Whiting, Indiana. By 1940, a number of industrial suburbs bordered Chicago. Railroads carried their products to the city and to the rest of the country.

Automobiles and the Suburbs

The automobile caused residential suburbs to expand. People built homes in the countryside and drove their cars to the railroad stations. They commuted by train to work in the city. When the roads to the city improved, and especially when the expressways were built in the 1960s, the suburbs boomed. People drove directly to work anywhere in the metropolitan area.

Expressways changed the suburbs in another important way. Businesses of all sizes were established along the busy highways. Companies from Chicago and from out of town moved to the suburbs. Land sites for new factories cost less in the suburbs than in the city. Tax rates were lower, too. In addition, plenty of workers lived nearby.

After 1960, old and new suburbs alike gobbled up farmland. The population of the suburbs skyrocketed. Some old suburbs that had about 500 people in 1960 now have 25,000 people.

Today, almost three hundred suburbs surround Chicago. The metropolitan area covers seven different counties. The suburbs have a combined population of four million people, compared to three million in the city. The population growth of the Chicago suburbs in the 1900s has been even more spectacular than the growth of Chicago was in the 1800s.

Life in the Suburbs

Like the neighborhoods in the city, no two suburbs are the same. Each has special features of its own. Some of the suburbs have ethnic neighborhoods. In most of the suburbs, people of different ethnic backgrounds live side by side. Suburbs have rich, middle class, and poor people.

There are several advantages to suburban life. Houses are usually larger than in the city and are not crowded so close together. School buildings are modern, and class sizes are smaller. Forty large, indoor shopping malls are located throughout the metropolitan area. People can drive to any of the malls and shop in comfort.

Suburbs are not free from problems, however. In some of the older suburbs, the housing is run down. Flooding is a serious problem in some places where builders filled in natural drainage areas to make way for new housing subdivisions, shopping malls, and parking lots. After a heavy rain, there is no place for the water to go except into people's basements and yards. Some young people think that life in the suburbs is boring. They get tired of going to the malls looking for something to do. They think the city is a far more exciting place to have fun.

Metropolitan Area Cooperation

The city, the counties, and the individual suburbs have begun to work together to solve some common problems. The Metropolitan Transit Authority coordinates buses and trains throughout the suburbs. This helps people get around from one suburb to another.

Many suburbs do not have enough water. The wells that supply water to the suburbs cannot keep pace with the increasing population. Minerals, such as iron in the well water, make it distasteful to drink. These suburbs now get fresh water from Lake Michigan after it has been purified in Chicago's filtration plant. A filtration plant filters out unwanted chemicals and minerals.

Cooperation between the city and the suburbs is important. Already the city and the suburbs cooperate to

remove sewage. The Metropolitan Sanitary District operates a canal and several sewage treatment plants. Usually, raw sewage is not allowed to enter the waterways. But people must work together to solve the many problems in the metropolitan area. Flood water must be controlled. Places must be found to put all the garbage and waste.

Shopping malls are a unique feature of suburban life. Woodfield Mall in Schaumburg is the third largest in the country (above).

People who live in the suburbs enjoy their communities. They are confident that the problems will be solved. Surburbanites have seen rapid changes since 1960. They are ready to move ahead again.

Culture in Chicago

Chicagoans have always loved fine works of art. When du Sable built his cabin by the lake, he hung oil paintings on the walls. Music, theaters, beautiful buildings, and landscaped parks help to make life in the city interesting.

Sounds of the City

More kinds of music are heard in Chicago than anywhere else in the United States. This is because there are so many different ethnic groups there. Each group has its favorite musical style. The kind of music you hear depends on where you are in the city, for Chicago's ethnic groups have not forgotten the music of their native lands. At weddings, neighborhood fes-tivals, and house parties, people dance to polkas, waltzes, or sambas. Many songs are sung in native languages. Older people in the neighborhoods teach the children how to dance to the music.

Jazz music and the blues were brought to Chicago by black people during the Great Migration. Chicago is known as the "Home of the Blues." Black musicians call the city "Sweet Home, Chicago!" Until the 1960s, only nightclubs and theaters in the Black Belt featured jazz and blues. Now jazz and blues clubs are located throughout the city. People come from around the world to hear this music. Rock and roll evolved partly from Chicago blues.

Chicago has several beautiful theaters and concert halls. Among them are the Auditorium Theater, Orchestra Hall, and the Civic Opera House. The Auditorium Theater is one of the finest theaters in the world. Orchestra Hall is home for the Chicago Symphony Orchestra. Opera singers and sometimes dancers perform in the Civic Opera House.

Art in Public Places

In cities everywhere there are statues of famous people in the local parks. Chicago is no exception. Over the years, the city parks and other public

One of the most famous of Chicago's public artworks is this Picasso sculpture outside Daley Plaza.

places have been used to display sculptures and statues.

Chicagoans like to pause and look at these works of art. They have three favorites. Augustus Saint-Gaudens's powerful statue of Abraham Lincoln stands tall at the entry of Lincoln Park on the North Side. A sculpture called *The Fountain of Time,* created by Lorado Taft, stands at the edge of Washington Park on the South Side. Downtown, people gaze at a giant sculpture in the Richard J. Daley Plaza. No one knows exactly what it is. People call it the "Chicago Picasso" after the famous Spanish-born artist who gave it to the city.

Chicago Architecture

Near the end of the nineteenth century, Chicago's central business district was filled with warehouses, stores, and office buildings. The district was surrounded by ethnic neighborhoods. There was only one way to expand— upwards.

Architects knew that the foundation of a brick building could only support about eight stories. A Chicago architect, William Le Baron Jenney, solved the problem of building higher in 1880. Using strong steel from the nearby mills, he developed a steel frame, like a skeleton, that shifted the support of the building from the foundation to the walls. His first steel

The curved surface of this building is a constantly changing reflection of the city's skyline. This building is one of many modern office buildings lining Wacker Drive.

frame buildings in Chicago were about ten stories tall. These buildings do not seem very tall today, but they were the world's first skyscrapers.

Young architects flocked to Chicago to form what became the Chicago School of Architecture. One of these architects was Louis Sullivan. He earned praise for the beautiful stone and iron details he added to early skyscrapers.

Soon, new skyscrapers shot up in downtown Chicago and in many other cities. Chicago architects designed buildings that reached to twenty, then forty, then sixty, then one hundred stories. Today, the city has several of the tallest buildings in the world. Sears Tower is the tallest of all—110 stories. It opened in 1975. Sears Tower

is actually nine separate skyscrapers that are bolted together to make one colossal building. Visitors take an elevator to the top of this building to get an amazing view of the city.

Electric elevators also made supertall buildings possible, and air conditioning brings comfort to the people who live and work in them. Imagine what it would be like to walk up ninety or one hundred flights of stairs on a hot summer day. Now, imagine what it would be like to work all day without air conditioning and then walk back down!

Many architects have followed in Jenney's and Sullivan's footsteps. For example, Helmut Jahn's buildings are covered with smooth skins of green glass. His State of Illinois Building brightens up downtown Chicago. Visitors and workers inside of the building can see the steel frames that hold it up. They can also see the the gears and cables inside the elevators and escalators.

Chicago's most famous residential architect was Frank Lloyd Wright. He designed houses that blend into the natural environment of the Midwest. His style is called the Prairie School because the houses are long and low to the ground, like the horizon on the prairie. Each of his houses was tailor-made for the owner. For example, doors and windows were made according to the owner's height.

Well-known landscape architects planned Chicago's parks. In 1909, Daniel Burnham laid out the plan for Chicago's green front lawn along the shore of Lake Michigan. City planners try to keep the Burnham Plan in mind when new ideas crop up about changing the shoreline. Other landscape

Famous architect Frank Lloyd Wright's (above) influence can be seen throughout the city. An example of his work is shown below.

architects designed broad boulevards that link the city's parks into two complete systems, one on the South Side and one on the North Side.

Chicago Writers

From its earliest days, Chicagoans have written about the city and its people. In 1856, Juliette Kinzie wrote a novel about the pioneers who came to Chicago. Her book was entitled *Wau-Bun.* Since then, dozens of famous authors have found plenty to write about in Chicago.

Some of the writers of the reform era were called muckrakers. They wrote about the problems of city life. Upton Sinclair wrote *The Jungle.* It described labor problems and unsanitary working conditions in the stockyards. Frank Norris wrote *The Octopus* about railroads.

Many of Chicago's best writers described life in the ethnic neighborhoods. James T. Farrell created an Irish-American character named Studs Lonigan. In several novels, Farrell told the history of Studs's family. Another novelist, Saul Bellow, created a character named Augie March, a young Jewish man on the North Side. Richard Wright's shocking novels describe how racism affected black people. Edna Ferber's *So Big* is about immigrants who settled in the suburb of South Holland.

Some of Chicago's best writing has appeared in newspapers. Two columnists stand out. Both Finley Peter Dunne in the past and Mike Royko today represent the use of humor and ethnic characters to comment on serious issues in the city. Dunne gave his point of view through Mr. Dooley, a South Side Irish-American. Royko

Chicago's writers reveal the lives of working people. The books of Studs Terkel let ordinary people tell their own stories.

Joan Shaffer

uses Slats Grobnik, a North Side Polish-American, to express his opinions.

Two great poets were inspired by Chicago. Gwendolyn Brooks writes about her experiences as a young girl in Bronzeville, her term for the Black Belt. Because of her prize-winning poems, Brooks was named poet laureate, or official poet, for the state of Illinois.

Carl Sandburg is another poet who lived in Chicago. In 1914, he sent a poem entitled "Chicago" to Harriet Monroe, the publisher of *Poetry* magazine. It became the most famous poem ever written about any United States city. Here is part of it:

Chicago
Hog butcher of the World,
Tool Maker, Stacker of Wheat,
Player with Railroads and the
    Nation's Freight Handler;
Stormy, husky, brawling,
City of the Big Shoulders: . . .

Fierce as a dog with tongue
    lapping for action, cunning as a
    savage pitted against the
    wilderness,
        Bareheaded,
        Shoveling,
        Wrecking,
        Planning,
        Building, breaking,
        rebuilding,

Carl Sandburg's poetry also dealt with the theme of the common person.

Under the smoke, dust all over
    his mouth, laughing with white
    teeth,
Under the terrible burden of
    destiny laughing as a young
    man laughs,
Laughing even as an ignorant
    fighter laughs who has never
    lost a battle,
Bragging and laughing that under
    his wrist is the pulse, and under
    his ribs the heart of the people,
        Laughing!
Laughing the stormy, husky,
    brawling laughter of Youth,
    half naked, sweating, proud to
    be Hog Butcher, Tool Maker,
    Stacker of Wheat, Player with
    Railroads and Freight Handler
    to the Nation.

WORLD CITIES

Chicago Is Your Kind of Town

Chicago offers plenty of things to see and do. If you visited the city, you could spend a quiet summer day on a beach along Lake Michigan. Or you could spend an exciting winter night watching professional basketball or hockey at Chicago Stadium. Year round, there is something for everyone in Chicago.

Chicago's Museums

Chicago has wonderful museums. Three of them are located in buildings that were part of the World's Columbian Exposition.

One of these is the Art Institute of Chicago on Michigan Avenue. You can recognize the building by its entrance which is guarded by two bronze lions. The Art Institute has a collection of paintings, sculptures, and other works of art from around the world. Chicagoans are especially proud of the French impressionist paintings from the 1880s that are on display in the galleries.

A little more than a mile south of the Art Institute is the Field Museum of Natural History, which has several sections. For example, in one section there are scenes showing what life was like in Indian villages and on Pacific islands. In another section, the museum features thousands of animals from around the world, which are mounted in realistic poses. If you visit the Field Museum, be sure to see the elephants and the dinosaur skeletons.

Founded in 1893, the Field Museum of Natural History features exhibits on both the animal world and human civilizations.

The Museum of Science and Industry is located farther south. It is the most popular museum in Chicago. More than four million people visit this museum every year. It has exhibits that explain how technology affects people's lives. Dozens of rooms are filled with all sorts of machines, from tiny gadgets to huge spacecraft. Like most Chicagoans, you will want to tour the U-505, a German submarine that was captured in World War II. You will also want to travel underground to the museum's coal mine.

Another popular museum is the Oriental Institute. This museum is located on the campus of the University of Chicago, not far from the Museum of Science and Industry. The Oriental Institute is famous for its collection of historical items from ancient Sumeria,

Babylonia, and Egypt. Several mummies are also on display. The Oriental Institute also has a full-size model of an ancient Egyptian house. Towering statues of the boy pharaoh, King Tutankhamen, and a great, winged Assyrian bull stand nearby.

The Chicago Historical Society is located in Lincoln Park on the North Side. All important books, documents, and records about the city are in the society's library. Dozens of exhibits show the city's history from the days of Fort Dearborn up to the present. When you want to know about the history of Chicago, you can find all the answers to your questions here.

There are many other museums to visit in Chicago. One features the history of medicine. Another shows what prehistoric plants and animals were

At Wrigley Field, Chicago baseball fans can cheer for the hometown Chicago Cubs.

like. Many of the ethnic neighborhoods have small museums and historical societies of their own.

The Sports Scene

Sports are another big pastime in Chicago. Chicagoans can watch their favorite teams or play their favorite sports with their friends. There are professional teams, college teams, school teams, and neighborhood leagues.

Professional sports follow one after another during the year. During baseball season in the spring and summer, the Cubs play at Wrigley Field and the White Sox play at Comiskey Park. In the fall, the Bears play football at Soldier Field. In winter, the Bulls play

basketball and the Black Hawks play hockey at Chicago Stadium.

Many Chicagoans cheer their favorite university teams, such as the Loyola University Ramblers or the Chicago State University Cougars. Small colleges, as well as high schools and elementary schools, have loyal fans, too. With 250 high schools and 1,500 elementary schools in the metropolitan area, there are plenty of teams to cheer.

You can play almost any sport you can think of in Chicago. Swimming and canoeing, golf and tennis, horseback riding and jogging, skydiving and kite-flying—Chicago has a place for these and many more.

Fields and Streams

Chicagoans like to spend time enjoying the natural environment in and around the city. They want to preserve what is left so people in the future can enjoy the natural sites.

Chicagoans like to have fun on Lake Michigan and on the rivers that flow through the metropolitan area. Only a few years ago, the waterways were polluted. Scientists feared that the lakes and rivers would never recover their health. Laws were passed to prevent more pollution. People can still swim, fish, and hike along riverbanks or sand dunes. Chicagoans are now on guard to protect the waterways from more harm.

The wetlands are also an important natural resource. Early in the city's history, the wetlands were thought to be unimportant. The city filled most of the wetlands near Lake Michigan with garbage. Today, people understand that the wetlands provide homes and nesting places for animals and birds. Rare plants grow there. On the outskirts of the city and in the suburbs, forest preserve districts protect the woodlands and wetlands. Here and there in the metropolitan area, it is still possible to see the place the Indians called *Checagou* some two hundred years ago.

Visiting Chicago's Historic Sites

Downtown Chicago has many historic sites because that is where the city was born. The outline of old Fort Dearborn is marked in the streets near the Chicago River. World famous buildings such as the John Hancock Center, Sears Tower, and Marina City are not far away. The area inside the Loop in downtown Chicago is dotted with brass plaques. They mark the site of the first school, the first city hall, the first church, the first synagogue. The Loop itself is famous. It refers to the central business district, around which runs the tracks of the "L." The "L" is an elevated train which is part of the city's transportation system.

Only a few years ago, Chicago's beaches were too polluted for swimming. Now, cleanup efforts have once again opened these areas for public use.

Still in use, the Illinois and Michigan Canal is now the centerpiece of the I&M National Heritage Corridor. This park runs along both sides of the waterway. It preserves sites from nineteenth-century canal days.

Aside from the downtown area, there are many other historic sites. Haymarket Square, west of downtown, was the scene of a violent battle between workers and police in 1886. When a bomb exploded during a labor rally, many people were hurt. Several people died. South of downtown is the University of Chicago, which is also an important historic site. During World War II, scientists worked in a secret laboratory under the stands of the school's football field. There they made the first atomic reactor that set off the nuclear age in 1942. Finally, even more south is the neighborhood of Pullman. The entire neighborhood is a historic district. Its factories were famous the world over.

The suburbs also have historic sites. The Illinois and Michigan Canal is now a historic corridor about 70 miles (113 km) long and 50 feet (15 m) wide. There is no historic site like it anywhere in the United States. Every suburb has some historic place that helps its new residents learn about the town's past. Many towns have restored the oldest neighborhoods and buildings that recall the days when the towns were tiny farming communities. People who remember those days work to preserve that part of surburban history.

WORLD
CITIES

Chicago in the Twenty-first Century

What lies ahead for Chicago and the metropolitan area? How will the city plan for the future? Will people continue to come to Chicago to live and visit? Will the city change as rapidly in the future as it has in the past?

Planning for the Future

Chicago has a tradition of planning. This tradition may have started with Daniel Burnham, the architect who was involved in the development of Chicago. Burnham taught Chicagoans how to think when they planned for the future. In 1909 he wrote:

Make no little plans; they have no magic to stir men's blood and probably will not be realized.

Make big plans, aim high in hope and worth, remembering that a noble, logical diagram once recorded will never die, but long after we are gone will be a living thing, asserting itself with ever-growing insistency. Remember that our sons and grandsons are going to do things that would stagger us.

Today, many city planners in Chicago are looking to the future. Some planning groups are concerned about only one issue in one area of the city. There are separate planning groups for the future of the Chicago River, Lake Michigan, and the wetlands. Other groups are concerned about several issues. They prepare for future changes in factories, businesses, and housing that will affect Chicago's neighborhoods. Still other groups make plans for the entire metropolitan area. Chicago's future depends on how well all these different groups cooperate.

Once a city of steel mills and stockyards, Chicago has become the world's leading producer of electrical machines and tools. It is still the world's railroad center, and the lake port is busy. O'Hare International Airport is the busiest airport in the world. The transportation links to Chicago have made it the hotel and convention capital of the nation.

In the future, the service industry will provide many more new jobs for

Carlye Calvin

Chicagoans. People in the service industry help workers in other businesses complete their jobs. Important parts of the service industry are banks, insurance companies, computer businesses, and advertising agencies. Many companies in the service industry will probably move their headquarters to Chicago.

Chicago: A City of Hopes and Dreams

The suburbs will continue to attract many Chicago families who think life will be better outside the city. New immigrants are expected to come to Chicago. Asians and more Spanish-speaking people will be the most important newcomers. Once again, the

Chicago's O'Hare International Airport is the world's busiest airport. Every year, this airport serves more than 48 million people.

ethnic neighborhoods will change. Some young adults will move from the suburbs to the city in search of excitement, but the population will probably rise in the suburban areas and drop in the city.

Against the city skyline, Buckingham Memorial Fountain in Grant Park sprays a stream of water 135 feet (41 m) high.

Planners believe that as the suburbs push out along the interstate highway system, Chicago's metropolitan area will eventually touch the metropolitan areas of other large cities. The Chicago metropolis will become part of a huge Midwest megalopolis.

By the year 2050, planners predict that the megalopolis will extend from Milwaukee, Wisconsin, through Chicago and across southern Michigan to Detroit. From there it will stretch eastward to Cleveland, Ohio, and end in Pittsburgh, Pennsylvania. By then the Chicago area will probably have ten million people.

As Chicagoans look ahead, they are confident. They remember how the city's people solved problems in the early days. They remember how the city recovered after the Great Chicago Fire. They know that the city still has many problems to solve. But they also will remember the words of Daniel Burnham: "Make no little plans."

Chicago: Historical Events

1673 The explorers Pere Jacques Marquette and Louis Jolliet travel over the site of the future city of Chicago.

1770s Jean Baptiste Point du Sable, a black fur trader, builds a trading post on the Chicago site.

1803 Fort Dearborn is built.

1812 Potawatomi Indians attack Fort Dearborn, killing many settlers and destroying the fort.

1818 Illinois becomes a state.

1835 Indians are forced to leave the Chicago area.

1837 Chicago is incorporated as a city, and its first government is formed.

1842 Work on the Illinois and Michigan Canal begins.

1847 Cyrus McCormick builds a factory to manufacture farm machinery in Chicago.

1848 The Illinois and Michigan Canal is opened.

The first Chicago railroad, the Galena and Chicago Union, begins operation.

1865 Union Stock Yards begins operation.

1870s Chicago becomes a center of iron and steel manufacturing.

1871 The Great Chicago Fire destroys a large part of the city.

1880s The world's first skyscrapers start to be built in Chicago.

1889 Hull House opens in Chicago.

1893 The World's Columbian Exposition attracts millions of people to Chicago.

1897 Elevated railroad tracks are laid to form Chicago's Loop.

1909 Daniel Burnham presents his lakefront landscaping plan for Chicago.

1913 Women in Illinois win the right to vote in presidential elections.

1919 Race riots leave forty people dead and five hundred people injured.

1920 Women in Illinois win the right to vote in numerous types of elections.

1933 The Century of Progress Exhibition opens in Chicago.

1942 Scientists make the first atomic reactor at the University of Chicago, leading to the development of the atomic bomb.

1955 O'Hare International Airport opens. Richard J. Daley is elected mayor for the first of four terms.

1975 Sears Tower, the tallest building in the world, opens.

1976 Mayor Richard J. Daley dies.

1979 Jane Byrne becomes Chicago's first woman mayor.

1983 Harold Washington becomes Chicago's first black mayor.

1987 Harold Washington wins election to a second term but dies in office. Eugene Sawyer becomes acting mayor.

1989 Richard M. Daley, son of Richard J., is elected mayor.

Downtown Chicago

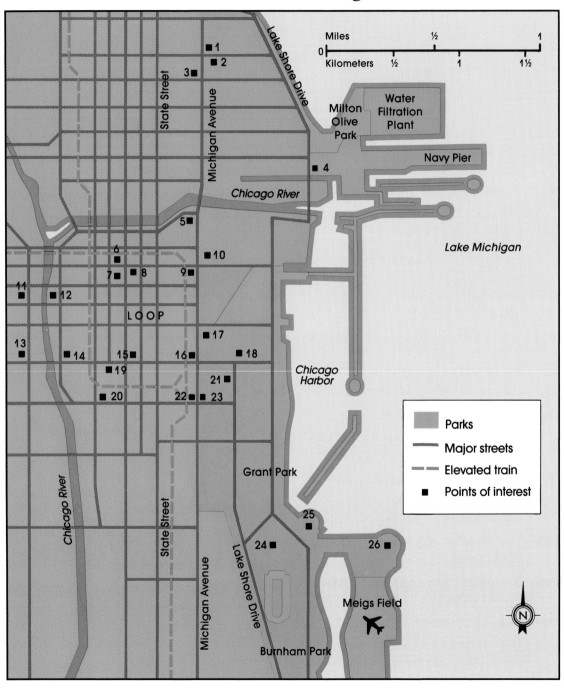

Map Key

Chicago Almanac

Location: Latitude—41.5° north. Longitude—87.4° west.

Climate: Continental. Average January temperature—23°F (-5°C). Average July temperature—72°F (22° C). Average annual precipitation—32 inches (81 cm).

Land Area: 228 sq. miles (590 sq. km).

Population: City proper—3,009,530 people (1986 census). Metropolitan area—6,188,000. World ranking—19. Population density—13,200 persons/sq. mile.

Major Airports: Chicago-O'Hare International Airport, Chicago Midway Airport, and Meigs Field handle over 48,000,000 passengers a year.

Colleges/Universities: 38 colleges, universities, and other institutions of higher learning, including University of Illinois at Chicago, Northeastern Illinois University, Chicago State University, University of Chicago, De Paul University, and Loyola University.

Medical Facilities: Hospitals—150+. Hospital beds—19,500. Doctors—6,900. Nurses—16,300.

Media: Newspapers—main newspapers are *Chicago Tribune, Chicago Sun-Times,* and *Daily Defender.* Radio—30 stations. Television—12 stations.

Major Buildings: AT&T Corporate Center—60 stories, 891 feet (271 m). Olympia Center—63 stories, 727 feet (221 m). Water Tower Place—74 stories, 859 feet (262 m). Standard Oil Building—80 stories, 1,136 feet (346 m). John Hancock Center—100 stories, 1,127 feet (343 m). Sears Tower—110 stories, 1,454 feet (443 m).

Port: Port of Chicago—29,870,000 tons/year.

Interesting Facts: The first skyscraper was built in Chicago. It stood ten stories high.

The world's tallest building, the Sears Tower, is found in Chicago.

Scientists at the University of Chicago built the first atomic reactor in 1942.

Index